ULIAQ'S Amazing Animals: Caribou

T0266425

WRITTEN BY
Danny Christopher

ILLUSTRATED BY
Amanda Sandland

Hi! My name is Uliaq. I love animals. One of my favourite animals is the caribou. Caribou are amazing!

1.7 m

Caribou are big. They can weigh up to 180 kilograms and stand up to 1.7 metres tall at the shoulder.

Both male and female caribou have antlers. The male's antlers are a lot bigger than the female's.

Did you know?
Male caribou are called bulls, and female caribou are called cows. Young caribou are called calves.

Caribou live in northern parts of the world. They have short but thick fur to help them stay warm in the cold Arctic winters.

They also have thick hooves to help them walk on snowy ground.

Caribou live in big groups called herds. Herds can have thousands and thousands of caribou.

Some herds are so big that when they move it sounds like thunder!

Did you know?
In the winter, caribou use
their sharp hooves to dig
in the snow for lichen.

Caribou are herbivores. That means they eat plants, such as leaves, grasses, and lichen.

Some caribou herds migrate. This means they travel huge distances together.

It is hard for caribou to find food in the winter. Moving south can help them survive the difficult winter months.

Caribou calves are born in the spring. They can stand and walk right away after they are born.

In a few hours, the calves can even run faster than I can!

Caribou are very alert. They need to watch for wolves nearby hunting them.

But if wolves start chasing them, caribou can run really fast to get away from the wolves. They can run up to 80 kilometres per hour!

Caribou get a new set of antlers every year! Male caribou's antlers fall off in the fall. Female caribou's antlers fall off in the spring.

Caribou use their antlers for protection. Male caribou also use their antlers to fight one another and to prove they are the strongest in the herd.

I told you. Caribou are amazing! That's why they are one of my favourite animals.

What do you like about caribou?